Llamas

Hello!

Camilla de la Bédoyère

Quarto is the authority on a wide range of topics.

Quarto educates, entertains and enriches the lives of our readers—enthusiasts and lovers of hands-on living.

www.quartoknows.com

Author: Camilla de la Bédoyère
Editor: Emily Pither
Designer: Grand Union Design

© 2018 Quarto Publishing plc

First published in 2018 by QEB Publishing,
an imprint of The Quarto Group.
6 Orchard Road
Suite 100
Lake Forest, CA 92630
T: +1 949 380 7510
F: +1 949 380 7575
www.QuartoKnows.com

A CIP record for this book is available from
the Library of Congress.

ISBN 978 0 7112 4100 8

Manufactured in Dongguan, China TL092018

9 8 7 6 5 4 3 2 1

MIX
Paper from
responsible sources
FSC® C104723

Photo Acknowledgments

Alamy Stock Photo: 24-25 imageBROKER; 29 Leon Werdinger; **iStock:** 11 NNehring; 12 Gannet77; 15 t JRLPhotographer; 20 Freder; 28 hadynyah; 31 t KiraVolkov; **Shutterstock:** front cover mariait; back cover Eric Isselee; 9 m Eric Isselee; 9 b Svetlana Foote; 8 t alessandro pinto; 8 b Iakov Filimonov; 7 bg, 27 bg GreenBelka; 5 t Vitoriano Junior; 4-5 Diego Grandi; 32 cparrphotos; 31 b J. NATAYO; 30 volkova Natalia; 3 bg, 31 bg TairA; 3 Lisa Stelzel; 27 r photomaster; 27 b SB Freelancer; 26 Liga Alksne; 25 r Irina Solatges; 23 mcjeff; 22 Volodymyr Burdiak; 21 SC Image; 18-19 AirDef; 17 Lisa Stelzel; 16 ChameleonsEye; 15 Harald Toepfer; 14 Pakhnyushchy; 13 a_v_d; 10 Ksenia Ragozina; 1 Ramona Edwards.

contents

What is a Llama?

A llama is a tall animal.

It comes from
South America.

Llamas are **mammals**.

All mammals have hair.
They feed their babies
with milk.

The Andes are big mountains in South America.

South America

ANDES MOUNTAINS

What do llamas look like?

A llama has a long neck and a small head.

It has four long legs.
Each foot has two toes.

Most llamas are brown, white, gray, or black.

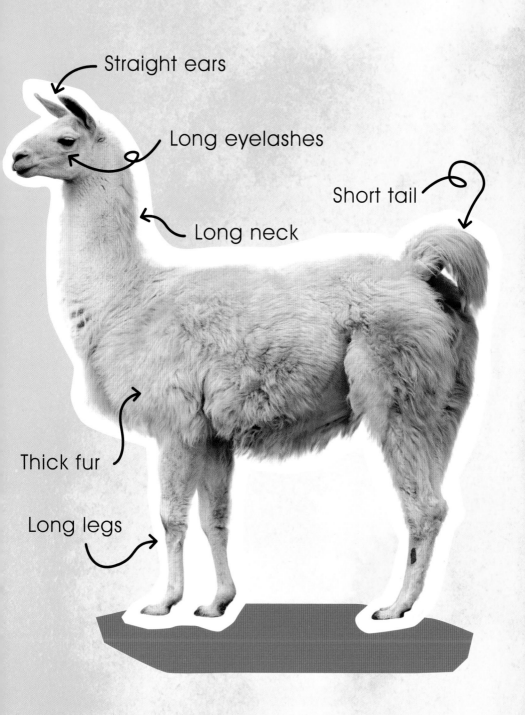

Straight ears

Long eyelashes

Short tail

Long neck

Thick fur

Long legs

Meet the family

Llamas are in a family of animals called **camelids**.

Here are the other animals in the camelid family.

Vicuna

Guanaco

All camelids have long, thin legs and long necks.

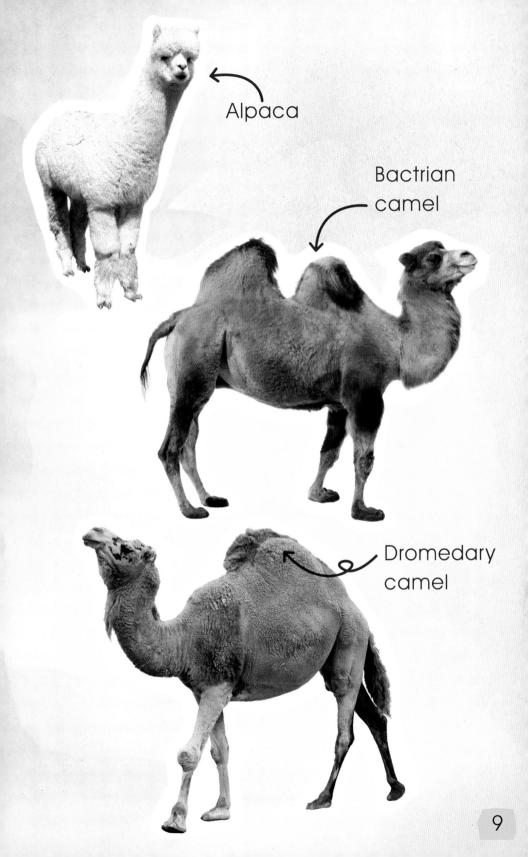

Alpaca

Bactrian camel

Dromedary camel

wild or not?

Some camelids live in the wild.

But most camelids are **tame**. They live with people, on farms or as pets.

Vicuna

Guanacos and vicunas live in the wild.

Llamas and alpacas are tame.

Camels are strong animals.
People can ride them, or use
them to carry heavy things.

Same or different?

Alpacas and llamas look alike, but they are not the same.

How are they different?

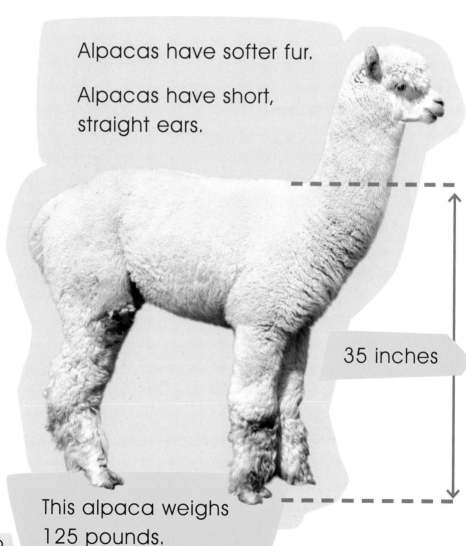

Alpacas have softer fur.

Alpacas have short, straight ears.

35 inches

This alpaca weighs 125 pounds.

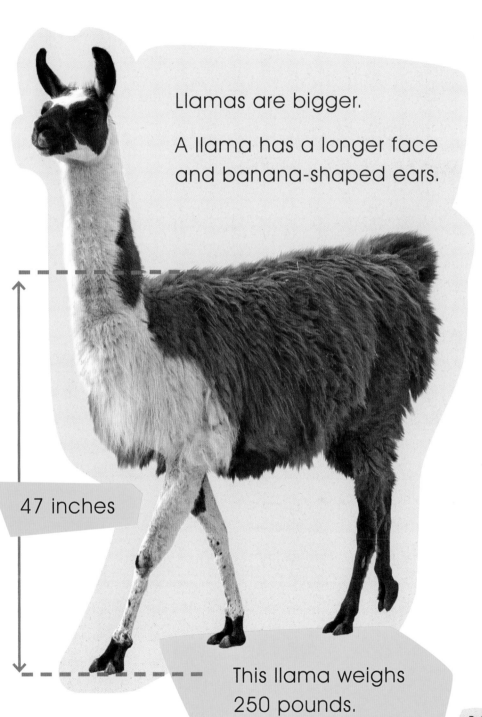

Llamas are bigger.

A llama has a longer face and banana-shaped ears.

47 inches

This llama weighs 250 pounds.

A llama's home

These llamas live in the mountains of South America.

A llama is **nimble**. It can climb on slippery rocks.

At night it is cold in the mountains. It can be windy too.

Llamas have woolly fur to keep them warm.

Llamas have small feet.
Each foot has a soft pad.

Hungry Llamas

Llamas eat plants.

They are **herbivores**.

Llamas have strong, sharp teeth to cut grass.

A llama has about 30 teeth.

They chew their food for
a long time.

They nibble
at leaves
and flowers.

what is a herd?

A herd is a group of animals.

Llamas live in herds.

There can be up to 20 llamas in a herd.

There is one father. The other adult llamas in the herd are mothers.

There are young llamas in the herd too.

The male llamas keep the herd safe.

Noisy Llamas

Many animals talk to each other. They use noises to talk.

Llamas are noisy animals!

They cluck, hum, and growl.

Llamas can spit, bite, or kick if they are scared.

Llamas make noises to warn others of danger.

Baby Llamas

A baby llama grows inside its mom for about one year.

A baby llama is called a cria.

Most baby llamas are born in the morning.

A cria can stand up when it is just 15 minutes old!

A mom has one baby at a time.

Why do people keep llamas?

Llamas are **pack animals**.

A pack animal is used to carry heavy things for people.

A llama carries things on its back.

A llama is a strong animal, but it is not strong enough for people to ride it.

The straps on this llama's face are called a **halter**.

Llamas and us

Llamas are very useful animals.

Llama **wool** is soft. We can use it to make cloth, rugs, and ropes.

Warm clothes can be made from the cloth.

Llama wool rug

Even llama poop is useful! It can be dried and burned for fuel.

Poop

Pet Llamas

Lots of people love llamas!

Some people keep them as pets.

Llamas are gentle, smart animals.
They like people.

Pet llamas live in **fields**.

They are happy to live outside.

They like other animals, especially sheep.

Happy Llamas

A llama needs friends. It likes to live with other llamas.

A happy llama has plenty of space to run and **graze**.

It needs fresh water and food every day.

Llamas need extra food in the winter.

Vets help to look after llamas.

A llama needs its toenails cut.

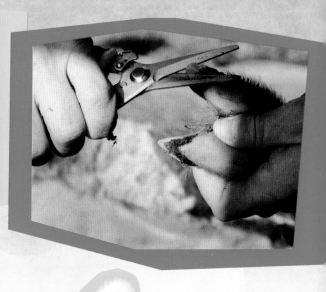

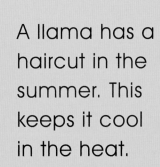

A llama has a haircut in the summer. This keeps it cool in the heat.

Glossary

Camelids
A family of animals with long, thin legs and long necks.

Field
An area of open land.

Graze
Eating grass or other plants in a field.

Halter
A strap placed around the head of an animal used for leading it.

Herbivore
An animal that feeds on plants.

Mammals
Animals that have hair and feed their babies with milk.

Nimble
A quick and light movement or action.

Pack animal
An animal used to carry things on journeys.

Tame
Tame animals are not wild. They live with people or on farms.

Wool
Animal hair.

Bye for now!